Social Direct Selling

Yes You Can!

(Book One)

How to Be Successful

By

Leigh Walton

Social Direct Selling

Yes You Can!

Book One

How to Be Successful

By Leigh Walton
First Published in 2014
Copyright by Leigh Walton

ISBN-13: 978-1503204829
ISBN-10: 1503204820

Why You Should Read This Book!

Leigh's personal experience of this industry makes this 'THE' book to read if you are contemplating or have already joined, a Social/Direct selling company.

Within its pages you will learn how to succeed and to increase your earning potential. Whether you want to earn a good income whilst working flexible hours, possibly part-time if you are a working parent, or to build your own team - which can provide an exceptional income - this book makes an excellent guide!

From deciding which company is right for you, to learning best practices, Leigh has got it all covered for you.

The down to earth and direct advice Leigh provides (and is known for) is suitable for those new to Social/Direct selling. Additionally it is a great resource for those with experience - but wanting to develop their skills!

The second book in this series 'Social/Direct Selling – Yes You Can! How to Grow Your Business' builds on this advice and explains how to develop a successful team and really grow your business!

Pre-Release Reviews

"At last - a truly sensible, comprehensive guide to running a successful direct sales business. Whether you're new to this fast growing business sector, a seasoned pro, or even a corporate trainer, this no-nonsense book will equip you with a simple system, structure and strategy for greater success and rewards. Leigh's years of experience shine through and her concise, easy writing style will ensure that this will become a blueprint for direct sellers to use themselves and for training within their teams."
Marie Burleigh - National Recruitment and Training Manager, Nirvana Spa At Home

"These books are ideal for anyone taking their first steps into the world of Direct Sales, but equally invaluable for long serving Direct Sellers too! They are extremely well written, straight forward and easy to follow. So, in a nutshell, read the book + follow the rules and tips =Social Direct Selling Yes You Can!!"
Jo Egan - Company Director

"Great Read! Tells you all you need to know. It brings back very happy memories of being fortunate enough to work with Leigh - but NOW the next best thing to that, is having this book, it's just like having Leigh beside me!! But for all newbies to the industry - it walks them through it - Step by Step!!"
Lindsay McEwan-Allen – Avon Cosmetics Area Manager

"A fabulously clear, concise, comprehensive guide to succeeding in an industry which is best kept simple. Leigh has written this in a way that can easily be read & implemented by the user or even as a Training Guide for those delivering training to others"
Vonni Steer – Director citrus7 Ltd (Supplier to DSA)

Dedication

This book is dedicated to the many Social/Direct sellers who have inspired me over the twenty plus years that I have been involved in this business - Daphne Jones who taught me the disciplines of the business and pushed me to over achieve my early goals, Paul Southworth who, without knowing it, set a fine example of never forgetting the names of even the newest recruits.

I want to say a huge thank-you to the friends who proof read and helped edit - Martin Lister especially - and to those who previewed chapters and encouraged me to carry on - Marie, Joanne, Carolyn, Sarah, Jen and Lynne.

Finally to my family for believing in me as a writer and my husband Tom, without whose help, support and downright directness (even through my tantrums) this book would never have been finished. He is now my unpaid publisher, senior editor, and agent!

Index

Chapter 1

Introduction to Social Direct Selling

When people say they have never heard of Social/Direct selling, I never cease to be amazed. Perhaps it is the term they are not familiar with?

In a nutshell, Social/Direct selling can be traced back to the early civilisations of Egypt, Syria, Africa and India. By the fifth century, the business people of Athens were effectively trading as Social/Direct sellers and were seen as 'big players' in the rich history of this profession. One term used to describe the way our ancestors' did business was 'Trader'. Some Social/Direct selling businesses still apply this term to their independent sales-force. In the twenty first century Social/Direct selling has become a huge, global industry - providing an excellent earning opportunity, and choice of lifestyle, to millions of people.

To bring you bang up to date here are a few industry statistics (provided by the U.K. D.S.A. 2014):-

U.K. annual sales total around £1.5 billion.

An estimated 400,000 people are currently involved in direct selling in the UK.

24% of these are under 25 years of age.

There has been a 29% increase of 50+ Direct Sellers from 2010 to 2012.

Direct Selling is the largest provider of part-time independent earning opportunity in the UK.

In addition for those of you who are interested in Social/Direct selling in countries outside of the UK:-

U.S. sales totalled just shy of $30 billion in 2011, with more than 74% of the American public having purchased goods or services through direct selling.

Approximately 15.6 million people are involved in direct selling in the USA.

Worldwide sales are also strong, with more than $154 billion in sales.

More than 92 million people are involved in the industry worldwide.

Approximately 90% of all direct sellers work their businesses part-time.

Can you see what a powerhouse this industry is? The Social/Direct Selling Industry of the 21st century is a professional, dynamic and flexible business, open to anyone and everyone, and allows those that work in it something we all want in our work and our life.... 'CHOICE'

CHOICE of when to work

CHOICE of where to work

CHOICE of how to work

CHOICE of who to work with

CHOICE of hours to work

The flexibility of this profession is second to none. Added to the choices listed above is the fact that, although you run your own business, (small, medium, or large is your choice), you are also working under the umbrella of a larger company which should offer you:

Investment in new product

Support

Incentives

Training

Remembering the acronym, **ISIT**, If you find that the company you are considering does not offer these four qualities then ask yourself:

'IS IT' THE RIGHT COMPANY FOR ME?

Work Ethic Required in Order to Succeed!

As I have already mentioned, one of the key attractions of Social/Direct selling is that you choose when you want to work.

However, there is a huge difference between the words, 'Option' and 'Choice' Although you can choose when to work, work as an activity in itself it is not optional.

Consider these factors:

1. Unless you work consistently (even when you have built a large team) you will simply not earn money!

2. Social/Direct selling is not an option for laziness.

3. Lazy leaders do not keep the respect of their teams.

4. Lazy sellers do not earn money, after all the commission on zero sales is...zero!

Attitude

The most important attribute you need in this profession is:-

'ATTITUDE'.

Of course, that is the right attitude. A willingness to learn, plus an open and positive mind, will set you up for **SUCCESS**.

If you are willing to put in plenty of effort, and to learn from others who are already successful in this business, read on!

Just for fun I have listed some of the attributes that are useful in this profession under the acronym:-

ATTITUDE

Assertiveness

Tenacity

Trustworthy

Independent

Teachable

Unshakable

Drive

Energy

Let me share with you some of the benefits that a Social/Direct selling business can bring. I have used **SUCCESS** here to help you to remember:-

SUCCESS

Sense of freedom

Unique business opportunity

Cash

Chance to be your own boss

Exciting new business

Self-confidence

Success

Social/Direct selling encompasses a variety of ways to sell your product, although some companies may have a preferred method. Whether you are associated with Party Plan, Network Marketing, Social Selling, or an MLM company, if you want to maximise selling opportunities I suggest you use all three.

1. One-to-one product presentations

2. Group presentations (commonly known as the Party Plan model)

3. Social selling via social media/social occasions

Note: The Social/Direct selling industry uses a register (jargon) as do many professions. Do refer to the glossary if you are unsure of any terms. Party Plan companies often use different words for 'Parties', such as 'Classes', Shows' and 'Trunk Shows' – I have even encountered 'Book Looks' for a presentation of books. Throughout this book I will try to keep to 'Product Presentation' for simplicity.

Chapter 2

What to consider when looking at Companies & Products

In order to really get behind your new business I believe **you** need to love, and have faith in, the product **and** the company. Personally, I have never been able to sell anything that I didn't believe would be a 'worthwhile purchase' for my customers.

What it is about the company that attracts you?

Are they reputable?

Would you buy the product yourself?

If the product is consumable would you re-purchase after you run out?

If non consumable is the product of good quality?

Does the product excite you? By this I mean would you recommend it as a 'must try'?

I liken products to films and books. If I find a book I just can't put down then I absolutely have to tell family and friends about it. I find myself saying, 'You must read this book by 'xxxx' it's a great story and I love the way it is written, I just know you would enjoy it too'.

This is how you need to feel about the product you are going to be selling, otherwise you will find yourself saying something like, 'I don't suppose you have tried this....'

That in itself is a negative start to a conversation and your potential customer will say, 'No and I don't really want to'!

If you have been using the product yourself then I guess you will already have belief in the product - there is nothing better than experience to sell (or 'recommend' if you prefer this word) a product. If you haven't used the product yourself then start to do so as soon as you can.

Another way of finding out about the features and benefits of the product is to talk to other users. Note down any information that would be useful to help you to sell the product. You do not have to try every single product in the companies range to recommend them. You can simply say to potential customers, 'My friend Jo has been using this for six months and says it is her favourite product because...'

Tip: When selling/recommending a product talk about the benefits of the product, not the features. An example is, 'The benefit of using this pan is that it's made of aluminium, so when on the hob the heat is conducted quickly which ensures even cooking', as opposed to, 'This pan is manufactured from aluminium which is very trendy and would look fab in any kitchen'.

Another important consideration is the price point of the product. The price may be a little more expensive than that of a similar product on the high street, as Social/Direct sellers are giving the customer a different experience; excellent customer service, the ease of purchasing in their (or a friends) home, a chance to 'try before you buy', and direct delivery.

However, if the price difference is too great customers may purchase once and then retreat back to their original high street store. If you can do a little research you will have your ammunition, if needed, when a customer asks why your product is more expensive.

A little quote for you to bear in mind is: 'Nobody ever bought a Rolls Royce because it was cheap'.

An example I want to share with you relates to when I worked with a kitchenware company. Our products were more expensive than some kitchen tool specialist retailers, but our products came with guarantees, whereas similar products available through kitchenware shops only carried a guarantee if the manufacturer supplied one.

Once my customers understood the benefit of the product guarantee, they purchased the higher priced product from me with the confidence that they could return it if needs be.

If you are selling a low priced product then you need to ensure you can sell enough quantity to earn the amount of money you need or want to earn. Usually these products will be consumables and once you have built a good customer base, as long as you service the customers regularly and build good relationships you will generate repeat sales.

Again, many Social/Direct selling companies guarantee their product, so even when selling lower priced products, if you explain to potential customers that for example, 'If the colour doesn't suit, you can exchange it', you are still likely to gain a sale.

The company you have been asked to consider (or discovered on the DSA.org website), may well be one you have never heard of. Most Social/Direct selling companies are 'best kept secrets', and, in most cases, don't have a tangible presence (retail outlet) in the high street. This is wholly down to the method of selling. Many people will not have heard of even some of the largest and most successful Social/Direct selling companies. It certainly doesn't mean that the company is one you shouldn't consider.

I would advise that one of the very first things you need to do is attend a local team meeting so that you can meet others and hear what they have to say about the company. You will meet people just like you. I have found most Social/Direct sellers to be ordinary, honest people just like you and me, so don't be afraid to go along and ask lots of questions.

Of course, the person who introduced you to the company will want to talk to you too. Have a list of questions for them to answer. It may be a good idea to compile your list as you read this book. If they don't know the answer to any of your questions then ask them to ask their 'up-line', (this will be the person that introduced them to the company or the person that supports them in their business).

You can also look the company up on the Internet.

Is the website up to date and easy enough to use? This is a good way to gauge what your potential customers first impressions of the company will be should they visit the site.

Do you get a feeling of the company from the website? Are they small or large? Do they sell Worldwide, where in Europe do they have a presence, or are they only within the UK?

Is it a solid, well established, well known company or a small, new (but inspiring and exciting) company?

Is the product current or a little dated? What is the U.S.P. (Unique Selling Point)?

You need to invest an hour or two of your time to spend with the person who has offered you the opportunity to join their team. Whether this is to attend a presentation of product presentation or to accompany them whilst they are about their daily business it doesn't matter, but do take notes so that 'you learn as they earn'!

This should all be part of your introduction to the company just as in traditional business you would have some sort of induction.

Questions to ask may include

Target market....gender/age?

Is it a collectable/consumable product or does it stand-alone?

How is the product marketed? Single or multi-channel (see glossary for explanation)?

Do you need a website? Can you promote your product on Facebook and through other social media? Can you align your personal website to the company/corporate website?

Does the company have a market presence already?

Do the products get promoted via magazines?

What does the company do with leads that they generate?

Who do they allocate these to?

Do you have a specified geographical area or can you sell and recruit anywhere in the UK?

Can you sell/recruit outside the UK?

Does the company have any online training videos or interactive learning?

Chapter 3

Getting Paid

Career Plans - what you need to know!

Career Plans vary from company to company. Sometimes you can be drawn to a company because of the perceived high percentage of commission paid on product sales; however you need to look deeper into the plan and the product.

Let's imagine you are looking at the plan of a cosmetic company who pay 25% commission. You then compare this with a clothing company that may only pay 20% commission.

One consideration is that clothes are a higher priced product - thus it may be easier to sell £300 of clothing than £300 of lipsticks. However, have you checked whether the commission is paid on the sale price (thus including the VAT), or on the cost of the product after VAT has been deducted by the company? This can make a big difference to your earnings; a word of caution - fully investigate the product lines sold by the company you are considering joining, and ask exactly which products carry VAT.

Another consideration is that you need to ask what the value of an 'average order' placed by a customer is? For a cosmetics customer it is possibly around £10 - £20 (at time of writing), and around £30 - £50 for a clothing customer. Thus your selling opportunities are likely to result in higher sales if you are selling clothing, meaning you may earn more commission. Conversely, cosmetics are more consumable than clothes so it could be that you achieve more repeat orders from your cosmetic customers than from clothing customers, resulting in higher sales.

You really need to do some research here by talking to others who are involved in the company and asking questions about average orders, customer retention and customer buying patterns.

The choice is yours to make!

Because there are so many factors to consider, I have listed some important questions for you to ask before deciding if the career plan adds up for you. Refer the glossary at the end of the book for any terms you are not familiar with:

1. Do the company pay commissions on retail cost of the product, or do they deduct VAT before calculating commissions and over-rides?

2. What is the percentage of commission?

3. Does this change when you reach a certain level of sales?

4. Does the percentage change depending on your monthly sales figures? Or, once you have achieved a higher percentage of commission, do you continue to receive that - whatever your monthly sales total?

5. Do you have to achieve a certain amount of sales every month before you earn commission? If so, let's imagine you need to sell £300 every month and you fall sick and only reach £150 sales. Do you forego any commission?

6. Do you need to place orders weekly, monthly, or annually to retain your business and the benefits that go with it?

7. Are there any bonus payments for consistency? For example, if you sell around £1000 every month do you get a bonus after, say, 3 months of doing so?

8. What are the rewards for developing your business? Is it necessary to build a team to earn a higher percentage in commission or can you do so through building your sales; or do you need to do a combination of the two?

9. If you decide to build a team and recruit people, what are the benefits to you? Do you get a payment for introducing each new recruit? When your team produce sales, what percentage of their sales do you receive for managing/supporting them? How many levels down are you paid on for doing so?

10. For each leg/level that you build, do the percentages remain the same, or do they increase/decrease as you build more legs/levels?

11. Do you get a percentage increase as you work your way up the Career Plan and gain a new title?

12. What are the added benefits (if any) of the Career Plan?

13. What incentives does the company offer? Do you have the opportunity to earn new product as they are launched, or do you have to purchase new product each season? Do you have the opportunity to purchase these at a greater discount than your usual commission?

14. What are the downsides to the Career Plan? Do you lose title and earnings if you fail to produce the requirements for your title? Is this instant? Can you re-qualify for your status easily?

15. Can others overtake/pass you by, or do your down-line recruits/sponsors remain in your team?

16. If a team member recruits someone and then resigns, does that 2nd level person 'roll up' to you automatically?

17. Can team members leave and then re-join under someone else - or is there a specific period of time that has to pass before they can join again?

18. If products are returned within their guaranteed period does this affect your commissions? If so, how and when are they deducted?

19. Are there regular incentives on offer and are they achievable?

20. How much notice do the company have to give you if they wish to change the Career Plan?

A few extra points to consider are:

What is the cost of post and packing for orders and who pays for this? Is it you, or your customer/host?

Do you have to deliver the order to the host, or are the products delivered direct to the host or to customers?

What are the costs of stationery? How often will you need to purchase new brochures/catalogues?

Do the company provide personal websites for their consultants/distributors? Is there a cost? Can you build your own website? Can you link your website to other websites that you may own or be associated with?

Chapter 4

Getting Started - Successfully!

First things first

Your first step will be to register as self-employed. This is very simple to do online, but I would recommend seeking advice about how to manage your accounts and your tax situation. You can find specialist direct selling accountants via search engines. This is well worth investigating as some business accountants may not have experience of the Direct Selling Industry.

In addition, do check out the DSA.org website for more information on this unique industry.

Social Media and its importance!

By setting up a combination of a Personal Website/Facebook Page/Linked In/Twitter/any other social media, you will be able to share your enthusiasm for your new business. Although it is best to market your business in a variety of places, don't bite off more than you can chew. I suggest you employ the services of a good 'techy' friend or seek professional advice.

If you cannot keep web and social media sites up to date with regular posts, then prioritise and try just a couple initially. An out of date site, or page, looks unprofessional.

You may want to start off with a business social media site like Linked In, in addition to a fun site like Twitter or Facebook (depending on which of these you can drive more traffic through). If you find these manageable then develop a personal website too.

When potential customers visit your social media sites they will judge your business on what they see. Out of date or inaccurate information can cause frustration and confusion; customers may get the impression that your business is not particularly well organised, which is the last thing you want!

Don't try selling through your personal Faccbook or Twitter profiles immediately – use these for promoting and marketing in a light-hearted and fun manner. These are very much 'social' sites – a lot of people switch off, when they look at Newsfeed, visit your page, read a tweet, and they feel they are being 'sold to'. However, I do recommend **adding a business page** to your existing Facebook/Twitter profile pretty soon after you get your business up and running.

An exception to my rule of not using personal social media sites for business is when you initially launch your business, as I see this as 'announcing your arrival' and thus marketing! This is a great opportunity to share your enthusiasm and excitement. I am sure you will be forgiven for sharing your launch with your social Facebook community/Tweeters on this occasion!

You could post something like:

'Hi All, I just wanted to share my excitement with you. I have just started my own business and am raring to go. I promise not to post lots of business stuff on here, do shout if you are at all intrigued about what I am up to, Jo'.

How to respond to incoming posts regarding the suggested 'launch post' above:

1. When you get responses/comments on your launch post you may prefer to Private Message (referred to as PM subsequently) those people, asking them if they would like to take advantage of your, 'quieter/early days', by having a product presentation of their own - it is fine to ask them to help you out by having one of your first 'practice parties/presentations'. Do explain that they will get a gift for doing so. Don't be tempted to tell everything at this stage (you can do so later on when the booking is confirmed and you are doing your host coaching).

2. If you are going to be selling on a one to one basis, you could reply to posts saying something like:

'Thanks for your interest in my new venture! I would love to pop in and show you (product), or you could come round for a coffee here. When are you free this week?'

3. To those who are a distance away from you, reply:

'Thanks for your interest in my new venture! Can I suggest that you browse my (or the company) website? Meanwhile, I will pop a brochure in the post to you and follow up with a quick phone call to see if you would like to order or discuss any of the products'. Please PM me your telephone number and a good time to call you.'

You are better to phone/visit interested people to firm up their booking; you can explain how your business works in addition to imparting the benefits of having a product presentation. When you are at this stage you really need to enthuse. Enthusiasm is infectious and this should ensure that they duplicate this enthusiasm when inviting guests!

An additional reason for a face to face visit is that potential hosts/customers are less likely to give you an outright 'No' as opposed to during a phone call, or via written communication.

When setting up a Business Page for your Facebook Profile use this to advertise events that you would like to invite your contacts along to. Perhaps the company encourages guests to attend team meetings so that your customers feel 'special' and can really get a feel for the company you have joined. If so, be sure to promote these dates along with those of any fetes and fayres that you are contributing to. Also use this page to post testimonials from customers and hosts – this way you may generate incremental sales/referrals/bookings for product presentations.

Tip: Ask your Facebook friends to 'like' and 'share' your business page to ensure that you reach those people that you would not normally have contact with. It is amazing how friends will help you by sharing your business.

I recently (January 2014) promoted a friends clothing party business on my personal Facebook profile and got her four potential bookings within a day!

Sites such as Linked In are more business focused and are great for creating contacts. You need to highlight the fact that you are self-employed. Tell visitors that you have opportunities for others to join you; this is critical if you are going to build a team - **which is the best way to develop your business and increase your earning potential.**

Note: I find Linked In very useful as a PR tool, as you can invite connections of people you know to 'link-in'. This spreads the word very quickly and I personally have made some useful business contacts through this.

Work your Website

Your website is a great tool for business. You can occasionally drive people to this via your personal face-book profile - but note the word occasionally!

With regards to your website, ensure that you keep it up to date, I won't apologise for the fact that I have already mentioned this! Even changing some of the images from time to time gives it a fresh new look. It is critical to ensure that out of stock or discontinued products are not showing or being promoted.

Have you ever been into a shop that had a great advert for a product yet when you go to the counter the assistant told you, 'Oh, sorry we sold out of those last week and are not re-stocking'.

This infuriates me, and it must be the same for many other potential customers. The next time I see an offer from that retailer I think, 'It's pointless going in because they will probably have run out of stock anyway'.

That is not a reaction you want from your customers is it? They would soon become ex-customers!

When you update your website monthly you also create an opportunity to contact your customer database. How?

Simply email them with exciting little messages, such as:

'This month's offer is not to be missed! It is one of my/my best friends/my husbands (or similar) favourite products....check it out!

New to Networking?

Here a few ways to build your network!

Look at networking like this - it is simply 'casting a net' to catch potential 'work'. You will already have a whole heap of family, friends, colleagues and acquaintances so these are the first contacts that you can pop into your 'keep net'. As you meet new people you simple add them to your network, keep net or contact list – whichever you prefer to call it.

You also need to spread your net far and wide and you can ask existing contacts to help. One way to do so is to send a personal message to those contacts who work in any kind of environment which employs ten or more people Offer to take your products in to their place of work during lunch-break so that other employees have a chance to browse your stand in their break if they so wish. You will need to get permission from their employer and stress that you will adhere strictly to the time agreed beforehand, so that you don't interfere with productive business time.

When you are approaching companies and organisations you need to sell the benefit **for them to them**. If you simply ask to go in so that you can show your product off, which benefits you, they may well decline your offer. You need to explain that it is an **opportunity for their employees** to be 'entertained' during their lunch hour. If you donate some of your commission in order for the company to raise funds for a charity/staff/social fund etc.

you are more likely to get a positive response. Take the approach, 'What's in it for them', and you will be more successful. Explain that you will be going along to promote/show your product but should people wish to buy you will place orders for them. You could even ask if the company has a favourite charity and offer to donate a percentage of sales made to the charity of their choice.

You will need to work on building rapport and gaining trust when trying to break new ground; don't just rely on friends to get you a foot in the door! If your personal contact doesn't have the authority to make the decision to invite you in, ask them who you need to talk to and make an appointment to chat to the person who does.

Networking to find new contacts can be a little daunting but needs to be done! Once you start down this track, you find it is actually quite enjoyable, and very beneficial to your business. You will meet people you would perhaps never have met through a home presentation!

Source local business networking groups like Breakfast Clubs and the Chamber of Commerce. Ask if you can go along as a guest to their next meeting. Hand out business cards to people that you don't get to talk to. When you do speak to people take the initiative and ask them for a business card. You can then call them a day or so after the meeting to say you enjoyed making contact and also to explore whether they are looking for a second income or would enjoy a product presentation.

Get involved in local table-top events, fetes and other community based events. Go along with a nice display of product, information on hosting a presentation and information on joining your business. Events like this should only take up an hour or so of your time but can assist you in building large customer bases, especially if you do a **free prize draw** so that you gain names and addresses of potential customers/hosts for future contact.

A simple draw form would look like this:

(Company Name) Prize Draw	Date

Name

Address

PostCode

email

Home Tel

Mobile

I would like to see a catalogue	Yes / No
I would like to receive free product	Yes / No
I am interested in knowing more about how this business could work for me	Yes / No

Best time to contact   Morning Afternoon Evening

Tip: If you can see the organiser of an event face to face, you are more likely to get a date in the diary.

Be Prepared for Business

Here are five suggestions for your first month or so of business.

1. Ensure you have a business diary/calendar and always make sure you are booked ahead for approximately six weeks if you are running a party plan type business. If you work mainly on a one-to-one basis, ensure you have enough weekly activities booked in to achieve the sales and recruits you want.

2. It is important to remember that you are going to be managing your business, not vice-versa! I have often worked with people in Social/Direct selling who tell me that they feel like a 'Headless Chicken'; this is what happens when you let the business manage you. In other words you are being reactive as opposed to proactive.

3. To be successful from day one decide when you want to work, then book appointments in to suit you. Each day has three potential working slots – morning, afternoon and evening.

4. Your first month of business needs to be well planned. You will have heard the phrase:

'Failing to plan is planning to fail'

This is never truer than in a Social/Direct selling business.

You don't need to be 'Business Person of the Year' and you don't need a complicated business plan to be successful, but you do need a **PLAN**!

5. Three simple but essential steps are required:

Plan - your activities/actions.

Focus - on those activities/actions.

Follow up - on those activities/actions (follow up is a key business activity itself).

Basic Planning!

When working with new or inexperienced Social/Direct sellers I have always used a simple business plan which should detail:

a. When you are going to work. As previously mentioned you have three work-slots per day, thus twenty one work sessions per week. You choose how many slots you want to work. If you work the **'traffic light system'** you could colour in your planner like so:

Green slots - are when you are going to work.

Red slots - are when you are definitely not going to work.

Orange slots – are for when you would rather not work - but if an opportunity arose to move your business forward, say a coffee with a potential customer/host/new recruit - you would book it as a 'work slot'.

b. Who you will approach for initial sales/product presentations.

c. How and when you will launch your business, and who you will invite.

d. Any company training sessions/team meetings you plan to attend.

e. What you can expect to achieve in earnings and other benefits (free products, incentives, personal growth, etc.) from your first month's work.

All of this helps you to see (it also shows your family/friends) what sort of effort/activities you need to undertake, how much time you need to spend on your business, and what the rewards will be.

Note: It is important that you put in 'enough' effort, to create 'enough' business to earn 'enough' money!

I cannot tell you what 'enough' is – that is for you to decide!

However, if your recruiter arms you with information on average sales, average customer spend etc., and helps you to write a brief action plan of what you need to do to achieve the earnings you desire, you will be able to work out what **'enough'** is for you.

Note: Chapter 1 of Book 2 (How to Grow your Business) fully explains how to devise an initial business plan/potential business plan.

As mentioned earlier when I touched on networking, you will need to build a contact list. Aim to reach 100 names. Start with family and friends and then move on to work colleagues, people you know through places like yoga/tennis/church/gym/college/golf/football. Even fellow dog walkers, social media contacts, neighbours and old classmates need to go on your list.

As soon as you come face to face with potential customers at product presentations, you need to ask for referrals. A referral is simply a person that they know who could be interested in what you have to offer. More on this in Chapter 1 of Book 2 (How to Grow Your Business)! Don't feel that you have to know the product or the business inside out before you ask for referrals, as you will miss out on many new contacts. If someone likes something enough to purchase it you can bet they will have friends who would be interested too!

All you need to do is, once you have finished serving your customer, just say something like, 'Jo, who do you know that may be interested in (seeing this product/having a presentation)?', then **w-a-i-t**. Don't rush them. If they say, 'Oh, I have no idea', have something up your sleeve to draw a name out of them. You could try, 'OK, who do you know that is a little bit like you... if you enjoy (refer to product or the fact that they have held a presentation) then I bet some of your friends would too!

Note: If you are given a referral, be sure to ask, 'Would you mind if I rang (name) to explain that you thought he might also be interested in…?'

Practise this activity now, make a call to a friendly person and ask for a referral!

Note: If your customer is happy to give you a referral, but wants to remain anonymous, then tell them that when you call their friend you will start the conversation like this, 'Hi Harry, I am sorry to call unannounced but a friend of yours told me you may be a little bit interested in (insert what the interest is). Unfortunately, because I speak to so many people about (interest) I cannot recall which of your friends it was!'

If you don't get a referral just say, 'Ok, if you do think of anyone would you let me know, and perhaps pass their number on to me – or if you feel more comfortable passing my number onto them, then that's fine too'.

When asking for referrals whether face to face, over the phone or via social media, be prepared to get perhaps eight, 'I don't know anyone', or 'No's, out of every ten people you ask. This is still a very positive result. Imagine if you ask one hundred people and find twenty new customers? That would be great for your business.

Social/Direct selling is a numbers game - **Don't Give Up**!

For each presentation you undertake your motto for future bookings should be, **'I am never through till I've booked two'.**

As for sales, these will be achieved when you demonstrate your product effectively.

Bookings for presentations - you have no choice but to ask for these; you need to ask everyone – remember, **'If you don't ask, you don't get'**!

Why ask everyone?

Imagine you are at a friend's house with a dozen or so people. The host offers six or seven people a biscuit and bypasses you. How do you feel? Upset? Annoyed? Confused? Left out? Exactly - this is why you have to ask everyone and give them the opportunity to say yes or no. It is simply not your choice; it is **their** choice.

I will cover all aspects of booking presentations in detail in Chapter 2 of Book 2 (How to Grow Your Business) but I really don't want you to miss out on booking presentations from your first few group presentations (a common mistake in this business). People often say that they want to get to grips with the product or with sales before they focus on forward bookings or recruiting. My best advice to you is to focus on recruiting and bookings from **Day One**.

Tips:

1. Ask if company training and support is available? Is there a cost for this? Attend as many training sessions as you can – there will always be something you can learn.

2. Ask if you can shadow someone who is already successfully running a Social/Direct selling business.

3. Ask the person who recruited you if you can observe them in action; ask them to observe you too to provide you with constructive feedback.

Chapter 5

What Next?

There are many factors to consider as you take your business to the next level. You will need to hone your skills and streamline your activities. Let's take a more in-depth look at some of those key activities.

Customer Care - What does this entail?

Once you have started to build a business contact list, you will need to ensure that you are meeting and exceeding your contacts needs.

Social/Direct selling is a 'tailor made' business and when you 'tailor make' customer care this results in satisfied customers which will result in growth for your business. Satisfied customers do a good job of 'spreading the word' as they chat to friends/endorse you on social media, which could bring you referrals.

We have three types of contacts:

1. **Customers**

2. **Hosts** –people who will hold 'parties, trunk shows, presentations, selling events

3. **Potential Recruits**

You will need to set up some very simple and effective systems to allow you to become a master of customer care.

Firstly, decide whether you want to keep your records electronically or on paper. I always find that people work best with systems they enjoy and are comfortable using. If you hate paper work use the computer and vice versa. The last thing you want is for customer care to become a chore – which will happen if you set up a system that you find feels like hard work!

One system which works well, both electronically and as a paper system is to set up a yearly calendar to include a folder for each of the twelve months. Then have three sections within each folder as shown below. January would look like this:

January (monthly folder)

Potential Recruits (section 1)

Fred Smith - quiet period at work

Jill Green - on maternity leave

Sam Black - going part time at work

This information should be interpreted as 'this is a good time for these three contacts to join your team'.

Potential Hosts (section 2)

Jo Blogs - will have settled in new home and want to show it off

Jack Brown - likes to have friends round after the madness of family Christmas and New Year

Sue Jones - always has group presentation in February half term

This information should be read as 'I need to call these in January to book February presentations/parties'.

Potential Sales (section 3)

Jade Young - likes a bargain and sale in January

Ian Moore - will need to re-stock on product

Jack Russell - collects product which is on offer in January

This information is telling you that these people are likely to place orders in January if you contact them.

In a paper system you need to have an index card or piece of paper for each contact to enable you to add notes as you make contact. You can then move the card from one month to another depending on the outcome of the conversation. An example would be if you spoke to Jo Blogs in January about booking a presentation, and Jo said she was sick but requested you call her back in March – you would obviously move her 'contact details form' index card/piece of paper into March. You can do this in an electronic system too by 'cutting and pasting' or using an electronic diary system.

From January's example illustrated above, you will note that some of the listed activities will have immediate impact on the growth of your team and sales (see potential recruits and potential sales sections).

The booking section has most impact on the following months as January should already be fully booked. However, if you have postponements for January you could offer a little incentive if a potential February host books the now vacant January date you want to fill. Something small, such as offering to take a bottle of wine/box of biscuits along to the booking can help persuade people - retailers offer incentives all the time to swell sales and it works. Ever bought something just to take advantage of the 'freebie'?

Using the system described, as you book hosts into your planner/diary you simply move their details to the relevant month in your system which keeps everything up to date.

As you chat to potential recruits if they say, 'It's not for me right now', you need to ask, 'When is the best time to speak to you again, January or December?' (insert month).

You then move their details to that month, which again ensures your information is up to date.

During conversations with customers if they tell you, 'Actually I still have plenty of (product)' or they say 'I don't need anything right now', you simply reply, 'OK, when shall I call you back? Would next month be good or shall I call you in six weeks?' Then wait for them to tell you.

This is all about giving your contacts a choice, and ensures that you are not asking closed questions. Closed questions give you a 'yes or no' answer which makes it difficult to move the conversation on.

Can you see that you are taking control of the situation in all three instances? You are giving them a choice and avoiding 'yes' or 'no' answers. You are asking what we call, 'open ended questions', see examples in Chapter 6 Book 2(How to Grow Your Business), which are conversational questions as opposed to closed questions which can only result in a 'yes' or 'no' answer.

All of the above suggestions work. But...there is no point in you handling the calls well, and then not following up.

Note: If you say you will call someone back, you need to call when you promised!

Call back!

Even - for a small order

Even - when you feel nervous about calling

This is effective customer care!

Question: How will you manage this level of care as your business grows?

Answer: As your business grows you will find you naturally want to build a team to help you. Most new recruits come from customers and hosts therefore you will lose customers when they join your team. This effectively frees up time which you can fill by looking for and serving new customers.

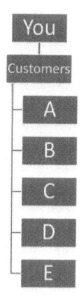

When your customer base grows so large that you cannot cope with customer care activities it is possibly because you are not offering the chance to join your business to your customers. Ask your up-line for help in identifying potential recruits from your contact detail forms or any customer record details. It is most likely that some of your customers already know each other and by recruiting one of these, perhaps ten others will be happy to be served by your new recruit giving you a smaller customer base to serve but adding a team member. The chart above shows you with your initial few customers – A, B, C, D, and E. As you build your customer base – F and so on – it will be natural that some of your established customers (having seen your success) would like to join your team and have their own business. The diagram below depicts this situation and shows that customers A and B are now consultants with customers of their own!

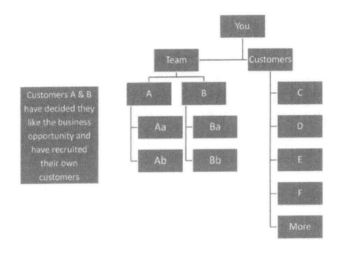

Generating Leads

Firstly, let's establish what a lead actually is! I remember thinking a lead was something with which to walk your dog. Joking apart, what do you believe a lead to be?

You possibly answered this with, 'A person who wants to buy product/book a presentation/join our business'.

Well, all of these are leads but in my mind I consider absolutely 'anyone and everyone' to be a lead.

In essence a lead is someone who may 'lead' you to someone who may 'lead' you to someone else who will be interested in what you have to offer. This is the same with referrals. If you only ask people to refer someone who is interested in your product you will most definitely be missing opportunities. After all, unless you have had a conversation with a person, how do you know whether they are interested in what you have to offer or not?

So a lead is not just someone who has expressed an interest – that is a 'hot lead', in other words someone who is actively looking to purchase! A lead or a referral is anyone, anywhere - though when asking for referrals it may be easier to ask your contacts, 'Who do you know that may be interested in (product/presentation/earning opportunity)?'

Often, we are tempted to assume someone we meet is either interested or disinterested in what we have to offer. However, as you may have heard before, assuming is making an **ASS** out of **U** and **ME**. When I first heard this I vowed never to **ASSUME** again. It made me a more successful lead generator and also a more curious person which has helped me in this profession. I question everything and everyone!

For you to enjoy success in this business model you have to continually find new leads. When you first launch your business you will initially probably feel more comfortable informing family and friends about what it is you do.

That's natural to most of us (although some of us prefer to approach people we don't know) but you can't depend on family and friends after your initial 6 - 8 weeks...unless you have an endless supply of friends and a rather large family.

What you can do though, is to ask them for help.

When informing family and friends about your business say to them, 'Who do you know that may be interested in...?'

A mistake we often make is to relay information about our business as a closed question (where we get a straight yes or no reply) such as, 'Do you know anyone who would be interested in..?'

When you ask this closed question you are most likely to get a simple 'No'.

Alternatively we use negative/nervous vocabulary and say something like, 'I don't suppose you know anyone who…?'

The common reply to this is, 'No, I don't!'

Although there are many ways to generate leads, simply asking for referrals or recommendations, as they are sometimes called, is the most effective way I have found. Think of it as seizing the opportunity at that particular moment in time. Sometimes people will say they would prefer to speak to their friend first to check whether sharing their details is ok but from experience I have not found this to be the case too often. Out of every ten people I ask, I would say around seven or eight are more than happy to give me friend's details.

Perhaps this is to do with the non-threatening and non-pushy way I present myself. I am always assertive and pro-active but never aggressive; I never put people under pressure.

When you are friendly, and your body language is relaxed and open, it is amazing how people react in a positive and responsive manner.

Consider these two conversations:

Conversation 1

A: Thanks for hosting for me today 'B'. Before I leave can I just ask who you know that, just like you have done, may like some free product for hosting a party/show/presentation?

B: Oh I really couldn't say. The only one of my close friends who wasn't here tonight isn't really into hosting this type of thing.

A: That's OK. If you do think of anyone just let me know, by the way the friend that wasn't here may still want to treat themselves. They may even know someone who would co-host with them, that way they could still get some free products. Would you mind if I called them?

B: No that would be fine, I hadn't realised two people can host together and his sister/brother may be up for it!

Conversation 2

49

A: Thanks for hosting for me today 'B'. Before I leave, can you give me the name and phone number of someone who may like some free product just like you will receive for hosting tonight?

B: Oh I really couldn't say. The only one of my close friends who wasn't here tonight is quite assertive and I couldn't answer for her.

A: Lots of people say that, but, if I tell her that you will receive a free gift if she books a presentation, I bet she will! If you give me her number I can call her now?

B: Sorry but I can't give out her number without asking.

Can you see how in Conversation 2 the Host must be thinking: 'Oh no, I would feel awful if my friend felt under pressure to book a presentation so that I get a free gift'.

From these examples I guess you can now understand how two very similar conversations, asking for leads, generate very different results? Gentle persuasion wins every time.

When asking for referrals it can help to offer a little incentive, especially when looking for business opportunity leads. I have always explained to people that if they gave me someone's details (name, phone number and address if possible) and that person joined my business I would reward them with a nice gift to show my appreciation.

This would usually be a product worth around £10-20 value as it would be worth that to me. You have to decide what you can afford if you were to use this method of lead generation.

For future bookings, the company you are working with will often offer 'Host Reward' systems and 'Booking Gifts' so there is no need for you to offer one too.

If you are looking to boost your sales, you could offer something small as a thank-you. Even a small discount off your customer's next order will suffice. For example, if a Customer purchases a product and voices that they cannot wait, 'To get their hands on it', ask them if they have any friends who may feel the same.

Say, 'If you tell your friends about this and one of them places an order I will give you X percent off the next order you place with me'.

People want to help and also like to feel appreciated – though not necessarily laden up with gifts! A little discount goes a long way – money talks, after all!

I used to keep a supply of chocolate 'Boost Bars' as an instant thank you. Telling people that they were helping me boost my business and giving them the chocolate always made them laugh; yes it may be 'tongue-in-cheek' but they remembered me!

Always keep in mind that this should be a fun business and you want people to enjoy chatting with you; you also want them to remember you!

A friend of mine in a previous business used chocolate to entice people to host/meet to find out about her business opportunity, during her group presentations. It went something like this:

If you are a 'Smartie' (hold up tube of Smarties') and want to find out more about this amazing business, why not take some 'Time Out' (hold up a Time Out bar) and meet me for a coffee or a glass of wine. I can tell you how this business has boosted (hold up Boost Bar) my income and given one of my team their confidence back after going through a flaky (hold up a Flake) patch. If you want to be 'star' of your own party (hold up Star Bar) then book me to come and entertain your friends whilst they shop from their seat and save their feet. Lastly, if you feel you deserve a treat (hold up any treat size pack of sweets) feel free to ask me any questions about products as you place your orders.

You may be holding your head in your hands as you read this but I can tell you, she got results! You just have to be a little cheeky and make it fun.

Elevator Speech

What you need as you go about your daily business is to develop what is called your 'Elevator Speech'. This is a two minute slot where you can tell people what you do in a nutshell – not just in an elevator but anywhere and anytime!

If you speak with enthusiasm and belief in your business you will find that this will help you to create enough coffee appointments to help with consistent recruiting.

Here are a couple of examples of an 'Elevator Speech':

'Hi, my name is ….. I am a self-employed team leader with 'Creative Cookware', (give business card), part of XXX group, (only mention this if your prospect is likely to have heard of them) who produce high quality, innovative and time-saving cookware and kitchen gadgets. We sell our product socially – often on a party plan basis – and not only do we have fun, but you end up with delicious food to share with your guests. The host gets a nice thank-you gift too! As a team leader I am also looking for people to join us and I have an exciting opportunity to offer. I would love to come along and do a show for you and your friends so that you can see exactly what it is I do. How does that sound to you?

The above was shared with me for the purpose of this book by an ex-colleague, Shirley Marelli, who is a Social/Direct Sales professional and has lots of experience and success under her belt!

'Hi, my name is Leigh, Leigh Walton, and I work with a company who have some exciting opportunities on offer just now. One is for people who would like to earn some extra cash –the other is for those who like to get friends together socially. This beautiful XXX that I am wearing is one of our products – the full range is amazing! I would love to tell you a little more about it, would you be interested in earning extra money or receiving some lovely free products?

I think you can guess who provided the second example! Do feel free to use these and insert your details - Shirley and I are more than happy for you to alter them as necessary.

There will be more on lead generation in Chapter 8, and also in Chapter 1 of Book 2 (How to Grow Your Business).

Following-up Leads

Confirm the appointment.

If you generate a lead for a presentation, or to meet someone to chat about the business opportunity, you should create the habit of confirming an appointment and writing it in your diary/calendar immediately.

If your prospect doesn't have a dairy to hand and so cannot book a firm appointment, ask them, 'When shall I call you? Is this afternoon OK, or is after 6pm better for you?'

If they say neither of these times, try for tomorrow. The rule here is to follow up within twenty four hours.

Why?

Because people go 'cold' - you can bet they will bump into (or speak to) what I call a 'Dream Stealer', pretty soon after you leave them. Dream stealers try to put others off whatever it is they are interested in; you need to ensure that you can 're-ignite the fire' and regain the interest of your leads as soon as possible.

I know of someone (who was extremely successful in Social/Direct sales) who used to leave her prospects with a pair of socks, telling them that they may 'Get cold feet' before they had chance to talk to her again and the socks were to keep them warm –this just created a bit of fun!

Note: Dream stealers come in all shapes and sizes. They are usually either jealous, negative nellies, or just insecure people who would love the opportunity to do something for themselves, but are too afraid to try it! Dream stealers may also try to put friends off hosting! They will say, 'Oh, I wouldn't bother with that, home presentations are old hat'. The truth is perhaps, that they tried to host a party in the past with little success. My guess here is that they were not 'Host-Coached', or they just didn't listen to the consultant's tips on how to get the most from your own group presentation. Or perhaps they are just not good in a social situation.

To be forewarned is to be forearmed. Your potential host/customer/new recruit will find they come up against people who say to them, 'I had a friend who tried Social/Direct selling and they just didn't earn any money'.

This will be because they either:

1. Joined a company where they needed to constantly invest in stock.

(If this is the case, or if the company you are considering/have joined ask for more than £150-£200 in the first month of joining, then do the math and ensure you can earn this back very quickly).

2. They were not taught how to work their business.

3. They didn't have support of an up-line and/or the company.

When addressing this concern, explain that is it natural for some people not to be supportive. Encourage them to try hosting/working the business so that they can experience it for themselves. Don't be tempted to put down the person who is trying to dissuade them.

Less is more.

Do not be tempted to 'tell all in a rush'. By this I mean if your prospect is a teeny bit interested in hosting or joining your team don't give them all the information on what the rewards are, how to invite guests, what to do about refreshments, how the business works etc. all in one mad rush. Enthuse about the key benefits of hosting a presentation/the business in general terms.

For potential hosts tell them they will have a fun experience but that you will book in a host coaching call to clarify everything. For prospective recruits explain that it is best if you book in a coffee appointment, so that you can explain everything that they need to know in detail. Make all calls and appointments within 24 hours to keep your prospect enthusiastic.

Presenting your Product – One to One!

When booking a one to one appointment with a potential customer it is a good idea to get a flavour of which products they are interested in. You can then take time before the appointment to think about which other products in your range would add value for them. I call this link-selling which is explained in detail in Chapter 3 of Book 2 (How to Grow Your Business).

Note: Don't feel tempted to start giving out lots of information until you have your prospects full attention and the time to spend with them. People are more likely to purchase when they are relaxed and fully informed about the product than when they feel rushed.

Presenting the Business – Practise makes perfect!

When first testing the water with potential recruit leads it is vital that you have at least twenty minutes of their time to explain how the business works and what the benefits to them could be.

Equally important is the fact that when you initially approach leads you don't want them to feel you are keeping information from them. I know of one well established company - who I will not mention by name - who are so secretive about what they do that most people find it off-putting. This is why it is beneficial for both of you to sit down over a cup of coffee where you can share your enthusiasm for the business, along with enough knowledge for them to make an informed decision.

I suggest that you practise presenting the business to family and friends who will give you constructive feedback on how you come across and whether the information is clearly presented to them. I have known people to practise on friends who they would not normally invite to join their business (that old pre-judging mind set is to blame here), and the friend has actually ended up joining!!

During the twenty minute 'chat and coffee' appointment you will need to identify your prospects 'hot button or buttons'. Hot buttons are basically 'needs and wants'. If someone is short of money, it is likely their hot button will be the need to earn money.

Take it from me - everyone has a 'Hot Button'.

Whether you have a customer who needs a face cream to give intensive hydration to their skin, someone who just enjoys the thrill of purchasing a new gadget, someone who needs extra money to pay the bills or even somebody who just wants a spare time job where they can meet new people - they all have a hot button.

When you press this button, you will achieve a positive reaction!

As a Social/Direct seller it is part of your job to identify these hot buttons; when you hone this skill you will find recruiting becomes easier.

Tip: Years ago, when I was a new Area Manager at Avon Cosmetics I was taught this little motto:

A A A A

Anywhere

Anytime

Always

Ask

This has stuck with me for over twenty five years and really has been influential in the success of my Social/Direct selling career. Even now, when I am in a coffee shop or a queue in the supermarket, if I can strike up a conversation with someone I hear moaning about their job, or saying they need more money, I will ask them if they have considered Social/Direct selling and point them in the direction of the DSA website where they can peruse the list of Direct Selling companies.

In fact, my husband and children have often said to me, 'Oh no, I can see you are listening to that conversation which means you are going to talk to them about X company/product'.

I find this rather amusing! I just can't help it - I really feel everyone should be offered the opportunity to find out about Social/Direct selling and the fantastic opportunities that this profession offers!

Chapter 6

Tools of your Trade

You! - Yes You!!

You are the most important and reliable tool/resource that you will ever have to hand. We all have two ears and one mouth and need to use them in the same ratio.

Why our mouth? All we have to do is open it and tell people what we do! Then we use our ears to listen attentively to the person we are chatting to and find out what may interest them - whether that is to purchase a quality product, host a presentation or earn money!

Simple isn't it?

So, why don't we inform everyone about our business?

Why don't we shout it from the rooftops?

Having worked with thousands of Social/Direct sellers over the past twenty plus year, I know that 90% of them will not have told **every single one** of their family and friends about the three opportunities they have on offer, which are:

To earn money - through joining your team

To save money - through hosting a presentation

To purchase product – where they receive a value for money product which they can return if it doesn't suit (via the guarantee)

If you had invested £10,000 in your business (as you would if you were buying a franchise, which operates in a similar way) would you have told more people, or invested more time in your business than if you had spent perhaps £150?

Why is that?

When I ask that in a face to face consultation, it often produces a light-bulb moment for most people.

They tell me, 'Of course I would have done everything I possibly could to at least make the £10,000 back as I couldn't afford to lose that much money!'

So why not imagine this is what you have invested and treat your business accordingly?

The Importance of Marketing

When you start your own small business you are the Sales Executive, the Marketing Executive, the Accountant, the Administration Manager etc.

The role of Marketing Executive is a key role, which works hand in hand with the role of the Sales Executive!

Marketing your business is an everyday activity - you don't have to have a complicated strategy. It can be undertaken as you are out and about, or you can plan in a few activities that focus solely on promoting your business. It is not a full time job, but it is an important one.

Here are a few ideas on how to begin marketing so that your business starts to have a presence in the marketplace:

1. Display a car sticker or car door magnet (companies such as Vista Print supply personalised door magnets that you just pop on car doors) so that you advertise your business as you are driving around. You may just be parked in a supermarket car park and someone may see your advert and give you a call! Even if they don't, this type of marketing/advertising raises awareness of your business.

2. Leave out-of-date catalogues everywhere! Just write on the front of them in a bold pen, 'Sample copy, for more information call…', and pop your name/email/telephone number on it. Leave them in waiting areas, such as doctors, dentists, hair dressers – the list is endless. It is best to check with staff that this is ok to do – just explain it's there for people to browse through whilst they are awaiting an appointment.

3. Scour community notice boards for news of 'events'. Events can be anything from a group who meet regularly and might want to book a speaker, (you can go in and speak about how you came to set up your own business and what inspires you about the product), to an Autumn Fayre/Spring Fete type of event. For fetes and fayres you would usually book a 'table-top' and display your product with the aim of attaining bookings/sales/leads. For groups who use speakers you would need to contact the organiser. If they say they are fully booked for a good while, you can either ask if they would like to book you at a later date, or you could offer to be a 'cancellation speaker'. These events can be great for generating business leads and, of course, you will most likely generate sales too if you enthuse and allow guests to try out your products. You could even offer to speak for free if X amount of product is sold!

4. As you meet people in everyday situations such as when queueing in a shop, at the hairdressers, whilst waiting for your children as they partake in activities such as dancing/swimming/gymnastics/football, find a way to strike up a conversation. A simple way to do this is to start the conversation with a smile! Your smile and your opening conversation are excellent tools that you will always have with you. The more you smile at people the easier it becomes. The more conversations you initiate the higher number of leads you will generate for your business. A simple sentence to start a conversation off is something like; 'Hi, I am Peters mum, Jackie'. It is pretty natural for the person you are talking to offer a reply. When they do so, take the conversation a little further by asking a few general questions such as:

Where do you live?

Do you work outside of the home?

How long has your child been doing (activity)?

Have you always lived in this area?

Then.....bring the conversation around to what you do for a living. Often you will find when you ask someone what their work entails, they will reciprocate and ask you the same question. Bingo...that's what you wanted. If they don't ask, you can just casually say, 'Have you ever heard of (your company name)?' If they respond positively, you continue the conversation by finding out what experience they have of the company and whether they would like to know more about joining, hosting or taking a look at the current product range. If they say they haven't heard of your company, you can still continue the conversation by simply telling them a little about the product and asking if they would like to look through the product range. If so, you need to get a catalogue to them and then follow up from there!

5. If you know anyone who is already involved in a Social/Direct selling business (however remotely you know them) contact them and ask them to have a presentation of your product. Even if you usually sell on a one to one basis you could offer to do a presentation of your product to a group of people. When asking other Social/Direct sellers to host a presentation, be sure to explain that you will reciprocate.

Note: It is simply unfair to promise to book a presentation and then cancel it. To this end I advise you to do your presentation first. There are a minority of unscrupulous people who will come and do a presentation for you and then they will not return the favour! To counteract this, do your presentation first and then be sure to honour your promise to let them come to you and present their product.

6. Use recyclable bags/bags for life with your business name boldly displayed. Many companies supply these. However, if your company doesn't I can recommend a company called Citrus 7 they specifically cater for Social/Direct sellers. www.citrus7.co.uk

7. Invest in a nice, well fitting, good quality top. I would suggest a polo shirt for guys and a V neck t-shirt for ladies. Have your company name and your website address printed on the back and be sure to wear this at events and presentations. You could even wear it as you are out and about to provide a bit of free advertising - it's up to you but if I were starting a business I certainly would!

8. Look out for any larger events suited to your product. For example if you are in lingerie, clothing, cosmetics, jewellery or accessories and you see a Charity Fashion Show advertised you could offer your help at the event. There are various ways to do this; you could offer to supply clothing and lingerie to be be modelled, or you could offer to supply make-up or accessories for the models. However, can you go the extra mile and:

a. Offer to supply models if they are in short supply (you will possibly have friends or contacts that would enjoy this).

b. Offer to help back stage applying make-up or dressing the models? The more effort that you put in the more you will reap the rewards. If you are in cosmetics offer to provide and apply the make up for free.

In addition make sure you have access to a well-placed table or stand where you can display your product and talk to people about bookings and business. You are not at the event primarily to sell - although you may generate sales and leads.

Note: If you are helping out at an event in addition to manning a stand, ensure that you have some experienced team members to help so that any potential leads do not slip through the net whilst you are busy.

9. If the company you have joined, or are about to join, provide leaflets on the business opportunity do ensure you have these to hand wherever you are. You never know who you may meet. I encourage everyone I work with in Social/Direct selling to carry a catalogue and recruiting information with them as they go about their daily business.

Why? Take these two scenarios:

1. You are chatting to someone in the supermarket that you haven't seen in ages. They tell you how much they love to use fragrance and candles in the home. You carry a range of these but don't have a catalogue to give them....What a missed opportunity!

2. You overhear someone saying that they need more money yet you don't have a leaflet to hand to them to explain about joining your business.

Get the picture? In both of the above situations you could:

* Help these people find a solution to their wants/needs.

* Help yourself by generating sales and a recruit.

The Telephone.

The phone is a key tool of your trade and not something to be (dare I say) feared! Many people state that they find it difficult to actually pick the phone up in the first place. If this is you then ask yourself:

What is it I am afraid of?

Why?

What is the worst thing that can happen?

How can I conquer this fear?

Fun Fact:

Fear is simply something that, once overcome, can be:

Fun

Easy

And

Rewarding

I don't know what your answers to the above questions are but having worked with, and coached, many people to overcome their phone phobias I hope the following will help.

Often we are afraid to make phone calls as we ourselves dislike interruptions at home and cold callers. However, if the incoming call was someone telling us we had won the lottery or even a raffle prize, how would we feel? Pretty interested in taking the call I guess.

The very first thing to do (before you even start making calls) is to ensure that you have informed customers that you are hot on customer care and you provide a 'customer care service' by way of calling most customers to ensure that they are happy with their product.

You need to do this when you take their very first order (usually at a presentation).

At the same time as you take the order ask, 'If I were to call you, what would be the best time of day and best number to use?'

Then tell yourself before you call, 'This is perfectly OK to do, as they have given me their permission...it is not a cold or unwanted call I am making'.

That covers the first two points - 'What am I afraid of and why?'

Now for the last two - 'What is the worst thing that can happen and how can I conquer this fear?'

The worst thing that can happen is that they either hang up on you/cut you short/say, 'No, I am not interested and please don't call again'.

Oh my word!!!! Guess what? You will still be breathing afterwards.

That old cliché, 'What doesn't kill you will make you stronger', is absolutely true.

On a serious note nobody really likes rejection, but in any sales profession whether you are selling recruitment into high-end jobs or selling a local charity magazine door to door, you have to get used to rejection.

It's your own attitude to it that counts.

You can decide to take it personally and let it knock you back, or you can take rejection in context and realise that it is not personal.

The other person simply does not want to buy, cannot afford to buy, or is not interested in the product you have on offer. That is their choice to make.

What you absolutely have to do (unless the person you have called just hangs up - which is unusual) is to leave the door open.

A closing comment from you also gives you the feeling of being in control, which is better for your self-confidence.

Thus, when you get a, 'No', simply smile (yes - even on the phone as this affects your voice in a positive way) and say, 'That's absolutely fine, thanks for your time and if you do need anything in the future please do feel free to get in touch'.

The way to conquer FEAR of the phone is to be aware of the possible outcomes and accept them as part of the job; then just make the calls. As the calls become part of your daily routine the fear subsides. Habit is the keyword here. I talk a lot about habit, the more often you do the activities that move your business forward the stronger the habit becomes. We need to develop good habits such as customer care as Social/Direct selling is very much a people business.

Another way to help overcome phone phobia is to add an element of fun.

Little things like putting a smiley face sticker, or a £££ sticker, on the phone itself can encourage us to pick the phone up.

Smiley faces are fun, ££££ remind you that each phone call could earn you money. For every five calls you make reward yourself with a little treat - say a mini bar of chocolate or a quick drink (hot chocolate on a cold day, fresh lemonade/fruit smoothie on a hot day).

If you do forty five minutes of calls reward yourself with a speciality tea or coffee/non-alcoholic cocktail/glass of wine/bar of speciality chocolate/nice portion of fruit salad...whatever it is that you really, really, enjoy.

Try and end your phone session on a positive call. If you cannot do this (perhaps you are making calls in your lunch hour and need to return to work) remember the importance of thanking the recipient and ending the call pleasantly so that you finish your calls feeling good.

Note: Never feel tempted to respond to a 'No' with a shrug of the shoulders and an 'OK' before hanging up. It's not good for you or the recipient of the call.

Tips:

1. When using the phone, if you stand up, you project your voice and have more control over intonation. This is because your diaphragm is not 'scrunched up' as it is when you sit down. It is also easier to breathe when you talk if you are standing up. Smile down the phone to your recipient. It really makes a difference. Practice now! Sit down, shoulders relaxed or slightly rounded, with a frown on your face and say, 'Hello, Leigh here', then stand up, head held high, breathe deeply, and smile and repeat. Notice the difference?

2. When using catalogues to market your business, fold the catalogue so that the 'front page' is actually the page that features the business opportunity . Most companies place the page that promotes joining the business somewhere near the front or near the back. To increase the chance of people reading something you want them to read, the front page is the best place. Emulate newspapers and magazines who always use the front page to advertise their biggest story!

As I have mentioned before, use old catalogues to distribute in places where people gather, such as dentists/doctors surgeries/community centres. Also use them to pop through doors, (do write across them in bold to let people know these are, 'Sample Catalogues', just in case they feature products no longer in stock/don't show up to date prices).

I can't tell you how many people have said to me in the past, 'I never thought to do that and I threw fifty catalogues in the recycling bin'. What a waste??? What a cost???

Fun Note: I am currently travelling Europe on a "Gap-Year". As a blogger I have nobody but me (and social media) to market my Travel Blog:

http://leightomwalton.wordpress.com/

Every camp site owner, every person I manage to engage in conversation (such as a tour guide, a neighbouring camper, or staff in the site shop) I give my blog address to!

This is marketing. It can also be labelled, 'Self-promotion'. To be a success you need to partake in this activity even when you are officially not working.

See I've even got it into this book!!

Chapter 7

How to Manage your Time

Work smart not hard!

Time management is down to self-discipline. If you constantly multi-task (and this is something that women in particular tend to do) you are likely to be a poorer manager of time for it!

You may be one of those people who undertakes many different activities in a day and wonders why others seem to work slowly!

If so you probably agree with this statement: 'I seem to be able to do everything quickly, and in between tasks I manage to do a bit of this and a bit of that'.

You probably also agree with this statement: 'I often feel stressed and under pressure'.

This could be because you are multi-tasking and might not even realise it. I am naturally that way inclined – but in order to work effectively, I have to make changes. People like us often don't take the time to think about how we use our time; we just get on and do what we need to do. However, when we take time out to think about how we spend our time, what we achieve, and how we could improve our management of time, we find we can decrease stress levels and achieve so much more.

I did a little research on multi-tasking with a group of very driven sales professionals.

When asked to reflect on a day's work, the majority reported they had done 'Everything to an OK standard - and ticked lots of tasks off their To-Do list'.

In addition they said, 'If I had made the effort to focus on one task at a time I would have enjoyed more job satisfaction, and more than likely improved my results'.

After a day multi-tasking you feel worn out by the sheer effort of juggling tasks and time. I consider this to be working hard, not working smart! When working from home it can be easy to find yourself working hard as opposed to smart. This can be attributed to having a less structured day than perhaps if you worked in a traditional office type environment.

During a home-office day when you have planned to make a number of customer care/business calls, when waiting for someone to answer the phone do you feel tempted to check your incoming emails? If so, you are multi-tasking but wasting time. You may wonder why I state, 'Wasting time'. This is because in this type of situation you will only be able to scan-read your emails, as your real focus will be on the call you are making. Thus you will have to re-read those same emails when you have the time to reply/take action. Can you now see that you are doubling up on this activity, and wasting precious time?

The advice here is to ensure that you set aside a chunk of time to work through emails when you have the time to digest the information and act on it. Otherwise by scan-reading emails whilst chatting on the phone, you may become distracted and miss an opportunity that arises during the call.

If you are making calls or working on administration tasks, ensure that your computer and mobile phones are in 'silent mode' and not announcing incoming calls or messages – this makes it less tempting to check them.

Tip: Set up your phone so that when you are focused on another task, or on another call, the answer machine plays a friendly message such as, 'Martin is on the phone at the moment. He will call you back as soon as he is finished if you leave your name and number'. If you can set your answer machine to cut in after three rings it means potential customers don't get frustrated like they do when a phone rings out for ages! You have worked hard to generate interest in your business - make sure you don't lose it through simply losing calls because you are too busy to answer!

Making Time to Work

You may have heard of Power Naps....have you heard of Power Hours?

A Power Hour is simply sixty minutes of time where you really focus on critical business activities. No interruptions allowed.

It is best to vary the activities you work on in any one hour; I wouldn't advise you do an hour of customer care calls, or an hour of following up on leads, or an hour of administration – that can feel heavy and boring!

Split the hour into twenty minute chunks. Use a timer to ensure that you move on to the next activity when the timer goes off. This way you are not tempted to carry on working on the activity you enjoy the most.

If you enjoy doing administration most of all (or your subconscious self says you do) then make administration the activity you work on for the last twenty minutes of the hour. That way you will get the money making tasks, such as making calls done too. I can't tell you the number of people I know of who have spent an hour or more just 'fiddling around'. At the end of a Power Hour ask yourself, 'Has that moved my business forward?' The answer must be, 'Yes!'

If your lifestyle doesn't afford you a whole hour at a time, use 'Chunks of Time'.

Always carry half a dozen Contact Information Pages*, a pen, diary pages or monthly planners to cover the next six weeks, information on any current host or recruit offers, and mobile phone with you wherever you are!

* These are pages out of your contact/lead folders if you are working a paper system. If you work an electronic system then your tablet will have this information stored. Refer to Chapter 5.

These should all slip into a brightly coloured plastic envelope covered with £££ stickers to encourage you to make calls. After all, any calls should result in extra income. When you have a free chunk of time, which could be in your lunch hour, if you arrive fifteen minutes early for an appointment, if you are on the train, or any other situation where you find you have perhaps ten or twenty minutes free time, then use this time to make some business calls

.

Any activity that needs investment of your time should be advancing your business, whether that is:

Arranging to meet a customer

Booking a presentation

Arranging to meet a potential recruit

Making an appointment to talk to a group or a charity about an upcoming event

Making customer care or follow-up calls

All these should result in income. They may not generate money immediately, but doing these activities **consistently** is the way to a **successful** business.

Contact information sheets should contain names, addresses, e-mail, and phone numbers for those people, along with any notes from previous contact you have made with them. It is wise to add 'best time to call' to ensure you call them when they are most likely to be available.

When to Work!

It is important to work when you are at your best. Can you answer these three questions easily and honestly? There are no right and wrong answers.

1. Do you know the best time for you personally to work?

2. When are you at your best and most alert?

3. When aren't you at your best? (most of us have tired and lethargic periods during our day!)

Did you answer :

Morning

Afternoon

Evening

You need to work when you are at your best (a luxury you don't have in a traditional job).

If you know you have a bit of a lull around 2pm (as I do), then do you think making calls or trying to present product/the business opportunity would be a good time to do so?

Of course it wouldn't!

Especially if you are yawning or tired; maybe you just feel a little dozy and can't digest information well? You will come across as not particularly interested, possibly unenthusiastic and a little dull. That's certainly not good for business and won't help if you are trying to impress potential customers.

If you are wide awake in the morning, then pack those hours with business activities. If you are an evening person then use those evening slots to make presentations and phone calls. Night owls could undertake activities such as updating social media, their website, and working on administrative tasks later in the evening.

Note: I suggest you don't phone anyone after 9pm at the very latest, unless they have specifically asked you to. Most people are just about relaxing from 9ish and an unexpected phone call may not be well received!

Taking a Break!

When you feel a little overwhelmed with your work-load (as all successful Social/Direct sellers do from time to time) take a break!

Just ten minutes away from your desk helps. Have a high energy snack and a drink, sit back and b-r-e-a-t-h-e. Set a timer and go back to work when the ten minutes are up. Prioritise what you absolutely must do and set aside what is not critical but needs attention. Anything that is 'nice to do' goes on the back burner.

When you feel you have so much to do that you don't know where to begin, it is critical that you take a little time out to get super organised and prioritise your work load! Don't be tempted to bury your head and think you will do it later – you will feel even more stressed. I promise.

Time Studies Exercise

I have included a time management exercise here for you. I take on board the fact that partaking in this exercise means you have to find the time to complete it (and you may feel you don't have the time to do so). However, it is **so worth doing**; when you review the sheets you will see exactly what you are spending most of your time doing. You can then assess whether this is time well spent or not.

Most Social/Direct sellers quickly realise they are either spending excess amounts of time on 'administration' or 'managing' their business rather than 'growing and developing' it. See how it works for you. Be honest with yourself or else there is no point in partaking in this exercise!

Please feel free to add to the following list of business activities that you undertake as a Social/Direct seller:

Making phone calls

Selling via social media

Host coaching

Product presentations

General administration

Marketing activities

Following up on leads

Next, produce a copy of the weekly planner shown below (this will be downloadable from my web site in the future) and keep this with you at all times. Fill in the weekly planner as you go. Do not wait until the end of the day! List the activities that you have undertaken and fill in the relevant time slots as far as possible.

Note: I have used hourly slots so if an activity takes you less than a full hour just make a note of how much time was used on the planner.

	Sunday	Monday	Tuesday	Wednesday	Thursday	Friday	Saturday
07:00							
08:00							
09:00							
10:00							
11:00							
12:00							
01:00							
02:00							
03:00							
04:00							
05:00							
06:00							
07:00							
08:00							
09:00							

Total Hours							

At the end of each week, go through the planner using the list below:

Checklist

1. Highlight each activity as Managing, Administration, or Growth. Use a different colour highlighter for each category: Red for Growth, Green for Managing, and Blue for Administration.

2. At a glance, what do the colours tell you about how you spend your time?

3. Add up the time spent on activities. Calculate the time spent on each activity separately.

4. Assess what you see.

5. Are you spending enough time on generating and following up leads (growth).

6. Are you spending too much/too little time on the phone/emailing and checking social media (managing).

7. How much time did you spend on 'administration activities? Was this productive?

8. How much time did you spend on customer care? Did this move your business forward? In what way did it move my business forward?

9. What do you feel was good about this week?

10. What would you do differently/what needs to change?

11. How can you focus your calls?

12. Can you eliminate some administration time?

13. Are you booking in 'follow-up time' after each presentation?

At the end of each week:

1. Recognise each of your successes.

2. Commit to implementing time saving techniques.

3. Believe in the positive results that you will celebrate next week as a result of managing your activities – instead of the activities managing you!

Now take a look at the Time Grid (which assumes a 13 hour working week and relates to a 'part time' Social/Direct seller). Does your working week look similar? Are you spending too much time on certain activities? Are your product presentations taking too long?

I have worked with people whose product presentations initially took around three and a half hours. After this time-studies exercise they trimmed this down to around two hours. You are probably wondering if there was a difference in the value of sales, number of future bookings made, and number of leads generated. I can tell you – there was no difference at all!

Activity	Time	Purpose
Host Coaching	45 minutes	Growth of my business as this ensures that my host knows what to expect and is looking forward to their presentation Key activity to get the most out of my presentations leading to potential recruits and more bookings
Interviews/Recruiting	90 minutes (min 2 per week)	Growth of my business Self-development via building my own sales team
Product Presentations	6 hours (3 per week)	Growth of my business Impacts recruiting/future bookings/sales
Follow up phone calls	45 minutes	Growth of my business – this includes: Following up on leads generated for presentations Confirming appointments for interviews Following up on interviews where prospective recruit has said 'maybe' or 'not now but call me in a couple of days/weeks/months'
Customer care calls	1 hour	Growth of my business as excellent customer care can bring referrals and additional sales from satisfied customers.
Administration	3 hours	Growth of my business as long as: I am marketing when on social media I analyse reports in order to address business needs (not just check my sales!) I only do activities that move my business forward or are absolutely necessary (not repeatedly tidying my desk)

To help with this exercise and to make it easier for you to analyse activities:

Growth is anything that is moving your business forward. A product presentation is classed as Growth if you book more than one new presentation and if you generate recruit leads.

If you leave a product presentation having sold product but with just one booking (which is replacing the

presentation you have just undertaken) then that is
Management.

Any appointments with prospective new team members
are Growth. Selling on Social Media is management.

Updating your website is **Administration**.

Chapter 8

Presenting yourself in Different Situations

Where do I start?

Most of us don't associate 'presenting ourselves' with interacting on a daily basis. We are more likely to link it to some form of public speaking. However, every time you meet someone - whether it's for the first time, at a social event, attending a business meeting, or in fact anytime you find yourself communicating with others, you are actually presenting yourself!

Thinking about this in simplistic terms, when you wake up in the morning do you simply fall out of bed and wander down to the local shop or jump in the car and set off for work? Of course you don't. You will more than likely do as most of us do - get up and shower, brush your hair and teeth, then get dressed. This is because we are unconsciously preparing to present ourselves to whoever we will come into contact with. This is why we think about what to wear – tailoring our appearance to our activities. For example if you were a Pilates instructor you would wear appropriate clothing, if you were a nurse you would wear your uniform. So if the idea of presenting (maybe even what to wear for the occasion) is scary for you, think again...you do it all the time. Of course, formal presenting is a little daunting for some of us, but you will need to learn to overcome this if you are considering a career in Social/Direct selling.

Did you know that the biggest fear, next to death, is public speaking? Yet Social/Direct sellers do this regularly without even thinking about it once they realise that 'public speaking' is simply talking to a group of people rather than talking to one person at a time.

Public speaking can be empowering and addictive. Anyone can do it, it just takes a bit of courage and maybe a little bit of acting. You will have to come out of your comfort zone just like many Social/Direct sellers before you.

Have you heard the saying, 'Fake it until you make it'?

The first few times you present your product to a group of people, this is what you will most likely have to do. Fake your confidence so that you come across well. You can say, 'I am new to this, so bear with me', but try not to come across as too nervous as people may think twice about booking you for a product presentation. So, stand tall, smile and make sure you continue breathing as you talk –consciously talking slower than you usually would helps! Practice your presentation four or five times before you go out and actually present to a group. Ask family or friends that you trust, to observe you and feedback. Don't ask anyone who is tactless enough to make snide remarks or laugh – these are usually dream-stealers. You know the type of people I mean!

A quick note on Personal Care

Guys! Ensure your stubble looks like 'designer stubble' not unkempt stubble.

Ladies! Long hair looks best when freshly washed and glossy. A must is to tie it back if you work with food. Even if you don't usually wear make-up, even just a sweep of mascara and a smudge of lipstick/lip gloss gives you a lift! Sorry but that is just the way it is!

All! Scrupulously clean hands, nails and teeth are a MUST, as is the fact that you shouldn't smoke before or during a meeting – most people really do not like the smell.

What to wear?

I will list a few ideas on what to wear for different business occasions, but I want to stress that whether you are attending a fairly casual meeting, informally presenting product in a person's home, or in a more formal business situation you need to 'dress the part'. On every occasion your clothes need to be pristine. Before you go out check for make-up marks around the collar, or toothpaste stains. Clothes that appear creased are not suitable for business wear, nor are less than sparkling shoes.....first impressions really do count.

Note: 'Coffee-to-go' often results in coffee drips on clothes - baby wipes are marvellous for this type of accidental stain. Carry a pack in the car!

For product presentations and informal meetings, where you want to present your business to potential recruits, you want to look smart but not too business like. I certainly don't recommend wearing a suit in this day and age. You don't want to scare people off. Casual, yet smart, trousers – for example chinos or very smart jeans - and an open necked shirt or similar is a good look for guys. For women, smart trousers/very smart jeans, skirt and top or a smart dress is fine.

I believe it is a good idea to invest in a couple of 'work' tops (as mentioned in Chapter 6) to wear at product presentations, fetes and other selling events. If you get these printed with your company logo, and personal website details, then you are a walking advert for your business. Team this with good trousers or a skirt; you will not only look smart, but you won't have to worry about what to wear, as this will form the basis of your business uniform.

Obviously, tracksuit bottoms, faded or scruffy jeans, creased trousers or skirt, are not going to inspire confidence in you or your product. Do yourself a favour and don't go down the route of, 'It's my business and I will wear what I feel comfortable in'.

For more formal situations, such as presenting at a team meeting or attending a company conference or breakfast meeting, a more business type outfit is necessary. This need not necessarily be a business suit – you could wear a smart cardigan over a dress or a jacket with co-ordinating trousers.

You will have attended team meetings by the time you come to present at these, so follow the lead of a successful team leader in the business you have joined. If you are to attend a local business group, for a breakfast networking meeting or business lunch, don't be shy to ask the co-ordinator what the 'usual dress code is'. These people are always happy to advise you!

If you are asked to be a guest speaker at a business conference a trouser or skirt suit, or a dress and jacket, will definitely make you feel more business-like and will project a good image.

Tip: Colour is important too!

Red projects energy, Yellow gets you noticed and gives the image of someone with a sunny disposition, blue is calming and not as noticeable (good for when you want to observe but not be observed).

Navy blue and black are 'solid colours' so can be good when you want to project a more serious image (that's why police and security workers wear these dark colours).

If you want to be the centre of attention at a team meeting go for a red dress or shirt!

If you want to simply sit back and observe others go for a shade of blue. If you want to present on a serious subject try navy blue.

Presentation Content

When you are presenting in a group situation you need to think about an opening, how best to present the product and how to close the presentation.

The Opening:

Let's think about your opening:

A. What does your audience want to know?

B. What do you want them to know?

Your audience wants to know five things:

1. A little bit about you

2. Why you are there

3. Why you are doing what you do

4. What the benefits are of buying your product

5. How much of their time you want

You want your audience to know three things:

1. There is an opportunity for them to do what you do - that is join the business/your team and **earn money**.

2. They can benefit from having their own presentation and receive host benefits such as free or discounted product - that is they can **save money**.

3. They can purchase from you a quality product which will have a guarantee (according to your company policy) - that is they can **spend money**.

Opening words:

Some Social/Direct sellers begin their presentation with what is often called an 'Infomercial'. This is basically a little bit of information intertwined with your own commercial - just like a television advert.

You could use something like this:

Hello, my name is Leigh, and I am here this (morning/afternoon/evening) to show you some fabulous products. Of course, I want to thank Jo for inviting me and to thank you for coming along. The product I want to share with you is sold 'direct to customer' rather than via retail outlets so instead of paying rent on a shop we reward our hosts with product. When you host your own party you benefit quite nicely!

I will take around 45 minutes to show you some of our products and then you can 'try before you buy'.

After the demonstration I will be happy to answer any questions you may have, to help you with your selection, and take your orders.

If there is a bit of queue forming whilst I am taking orders please feel free to glance through my 'boast-book' where you will see what my business has enabled me to achieve so far!

Note: A boast book (sometimes known as a brag-file) should contain personal and business information. Family photos, anything you have purchased with earnings such as a new car, holiday, chic garden furniture, along with photos of you and your colleagues at a fun team meeting and pictures of product you have achieved through company incentives etc. The purpose of this book is to encourage others to ask about your life and your work and to see that they too could achieve these benefits!

The Group Presentation:

This is where you tailor your product to the guests who are in attendance. If you have a group of people who don't wear make-up but like to look after their skin then focus on the skin care products. If you are presenting books to a group of people with toddlers then focus on the correct age range. If you have made focused host coaching calls to your host since booking the presentation, and know who her guests are, that will help you to tailor the product to your guests.

Because of the diversity of Social/Direct selling companies, you will need to speak to your up-line/company representative on how best to present your particular product. Some products need thorough demonstration and others need to be used (especially if you are demonstrating cooking utensils or cosmetics). If demonstrating jewellery or clothing you may want to show your customers different ways of wearing these products. The product presentation should last a maximum of forty five minutes.

Tip: People are likely to lose concentration during your presentation, especially in the evening when they may be more tired from the day's activities, so try to involve your audience. Vary your tone of voice and make eye contact with each of the guests at some point. You could make it more fun by throwing a sweet to guests when they interact positively with you!

Closing:

Here you need to round off the presentation and explain that your guests have three considerations which are:

Earn money - by joining you

Save money - by hosting a party

Spend money - how to order

You could say something like:

'Well that's my bit almost over. I hope you have enjoyed it as much as I have. Let me just remind you that I am here to help you to try out the product and to answer any questions you may have. I don't want you to buy something that you won't use regularly - I don't want you to waste your money!

I'm hot on customer care so I do make customer care calls, but I can't promise to call all of you. However, do not hesitate to call me if you have a query on your purchases, as I am your personal (insert company name) consultant.

I don't know if you can tell how much I love my job? (say this with a big smile) I am also building a team in this area - if you want a job that you could enjoy, whether it is to earn money, do something that is fun, or to build a new career, do let me know and I will treat you to coffee and a cake whilst explaining exactly how this business works.

For those of you who would like some free or discounted product, I would be delighted to come to your home and show your family and friends some products, so let me know and we will find a date that suits us both.

Lastly, if you just want to spend money - and who doesn't enjoy a treat now and then - I am more than happy to take your orders'...(again, say this with a big smile and with a 'tongue in cheek' attitude as a little cheek/flirting goes a long way).

The One to One Presentation:

This selling occasion needs to be less formal than with a group, although you still want to cover the same information.

I suggest you start off asking some generic questions about your potential customer. Have they tried the product before? Have they experience of a similar product? Explain a little about the way Social/Direct selling works, as you take them through your product lines. Note which ones they are interested in and help them to make choices.

Take their order, explain the guarantee and delivery and book in your follow up call or visit. Again, offer your customer the chance to do what you do, to earn money!!

Do not try to sell customers everything at once, but do not feel obliged to stop them buying! I once heard a story about a man in a clothes shop who, when his customer had chosen trousers, a shirt and a tie, took him to the cash till. The customer actually wanted a pair of shoes, socks and underpants too, but because the assistant 'assumed' the customer had spent enough, he had 'closed the sale'. If only he had asked, 'Is there anything else I can help you with?'

Tip: A useful phrase to remember is, '**Buy** the Way'. (note the misspelling).

When a customer buys a product, for example a pair of shoes, if you simply say, '**Buy** the way this shoe polish is anti-scuff and the exact shade of those shoes, would you like me to get one for you?', you are likely to build the sale. The worst that can happen is that the customer says, 'No thank you'. You are simply offering a useful additional product – the customer **chooses** whether to buy or not. Imagine if every single customer spent just £2 extra? If you take an average of twenty customers a week which equals eighty customers a month, that adds up to nine hundred and sixty customers a year, all spending an extra £2.

Your '**Buy** the way' (or incremental) sales would total £1,920.00 a year. What would your commission be on that? Certainly worth having!

Presenting at Fetes and other Events:

This situation is almost the opposite of being in a retail environment. By that statement I mean:

Retail -Waiting for customers to come to you.

Social/Direct Selling - Approaching potential customers with a warm welcome, a smile and an invitation to look without being 'pounced upon'.

Retail - Standing behind a counter – sometimes seen as unapproachable.

Social/Direct Selling - Standing to the side of your counter (table) - you instantly seem more approachable.

Retail - Taking the order thus closing the sale.

Social/Direct Selling - Taking the order then offering 'Buy the way' additional product which allows the Customer to 'close the sale'.

Some guidance on **Approaching Potential Customers:**

I don't want you to think you have to rush up to people, accost them and be 'in their face'. Like most people, I would hate that if I were a customer.

What you need to do is to stand by your counter/table, brochure in hand, smile at people walking by and open up conversation, starting with:-

'Hi there, can I just ask if you have heard of (insert company name)?'

Or:

'Good morning, how are you today? Are you enjoying the event?'

This gives them chance to assess what kind of person you are. A pleasant comment can create a non-threatening first impression which means people are more likely to stop and chat - and maybe ask you a few questions about your product/company.

When you are in conversation it is easier to ask if you can explain a little about your product and what you are doing at the event. Use the opportunity to explain that you are building a team, and have some vacancies.

Also be sure to look for presentation bookings when you are working at an event. Say something along the lines of, 'I come out to people's homes and places of work etc. to showcase my product. It's a good opportunity to get friends together for a fun morning, afternoon or evening - and the host receives a lovely thank you gift too. How does that sound?'

Another way to find business at events is if you are happy to fundraise for groups and charities. Ask visitors to your stand, 'Is there a particular charity close to your heart? I could come along and run a fundraiser for you whereby a percentage of my sales are donated to your charity or group. Can we make an appointment to discuss how I could help you?'

Bear in mind that fetes and fayres may not create immediate sales, although you may take some orders. These events are great for generating new contacts and recruit leads. In addition they can help you to gain bookings and appointments for future selling opportunities. It is essential for you to take names, addresses (postal or email), and phone numbers of people who visit your stand and show interest in your product. Otherwise, how can you follow up effectively?

One way of doing this easily is to have a 'Free Prize Draw', refer to Chapter 4 for an example of a free prize draw form. You will need to provide a prize – product is the best for this - and it needn't cost a fortune.

It goes without saying that any leads you generate via your free prize draw simply **MUST** be followed up. I have spoken to people in the past who have said, 'Oh I left my details with someone from your company at the last event here but they didn't bother calling me'.

Not a good advertisement! If you don't do as you promise you are not only letting yourself down but also your colleagues and team members.

Tip: Less is more!

Don't feel you need to persuade visitors to your stand that they should be interested in your product/a presentation/the business. Give them the space to decide for themselves. I have seen many Social/Direct sellers 'ensure' that every visitor becomes a lead of some sort – only to end up with hundreds of 'leads' to follow up. I would rather qualify the lead there and then, and end up with twenty good leads than a hundred doubtful contacts!

Ask yourself: Do I really want fifty lukewarm leads to follow up on, or would fifteen hot/warm leads be more manageable and give me a better result?

Presenting the Business Opportunity

When you are presenting the business opportunity, whether to a group or one to one I suggest you develop, and stick to, a structure.

An Opportunity Brochure or Business Presenter is a really useful tool for a one to one. These are booklets containing information on the company and the business opportunities available. Some companies provide you with these. If your chosen company doesn't then it is a good idea to make your own (see below for ideas on how).

When presenting to a group, consider using either a well written flip chart or a simple power-point presentation which needs to contain the same information as in the previous paragraph.

These tools give flow and structure, ensuring that you do not 'waffle on' or miss out valid points. Using visual aids also gives your audience something to focus on, rather than feeling that they are being talked at! In addition they give you the opportunity to observe your audience throughout the presentation whilst they are looking at the visual aid and not solely at you. Observing your audience helps you to make sure that you are not losing their attention. Additionally, if you catch people looking confused, you can take a minute to check their understanding of what you are saying to them.

As mentioned above, if the company you have joined doesn't have an 'Opportunity Brochure' or power-point presentation already written, then I suggest you compile one which should contain the following information:

1. Company background

2. How and where self-employed consultants sell their product

3. Where and how to find business

4. An overview of the career plan

5. An overview of ongoing support offered by the company and self-employed leaders

6. Any incentives offered by the company

7. Next steps

All that should take no more than twenty minutes to run through with your prospective recruit/s. Then it is over to them to ask questions, and you to answer them honestly.

There will be more in depth information on conducting interviews and recruiting in Chapter 1 Book 2 (How to Grow Your Business).

Summing Up

This book has taken you step by step through the tentative stages of deciding whether Social/Direct selling is an option for you, and what to look for when you are researching companies that you are aware of.

You now have an understanding of how Career Plans work, and some of the many benefits this dynamic business can offer e.g. extra finance, fun, flexibility, freedom to work when you want being just a few!

I hope you are about to, or have already joined, the Social Direct selling business of your choice. The chapters on Getting Started and What Next have taken you through the early stages of setting your business up, whilst Tools of your Trade should give you food for thought – I bet you have never thought of yourself as a 'resource' before, but that is exactly what you are!

Social/Direct sellers need to be resourceful and energetic, and in order to be so, you must remember to take some 'me time' so that you can re-charge your batteries regularly. The chapter on Time Management should help ensure you work when you are at your best – only then will you realise great results for your business.

'Work Smart – Not Hard!'

The final chapter - Presenting Yourself – guided you through some of the different situations you will find yourself in and I hope the tips on dress, how to present and what to present, inspire confidence in what can be perceived as 'scary situations'. Remember – you already 'present yourself' on a daily basis – you just haven't thought about it in that way before, perhaps!

Finally, if you take just two things from this book, they are:

The four **AAAA's** – **A**nywhere, **A**nytime, **A**lways **A**sk

And:

Attitude – a **'Positive Attitude'** is the most important attribute in our exciting, dynamic profession.

I really hope that you have enjoyed this book, but more importantly, I hope that you use the ideas and the knowledge that I have shared, to create a business that will help you grow as an individual, and provide you with extra income!

Book 2 in this series **'How To Grow Your Business'** will explore topics such as Increasing Sales, Achieving more Bookings for Presentations, Building a Team and Developing Others.

In essence, it will teach you move your business to the next level of success,…what are you waiting for?

Have fun!

Leigh

Glossary

Booking

Creating interest in and diarising, a firm date for holding a product presentation.

Career Plan

Sometimes referred to as, the Marketing, Compensation or Payment Plan. This explains what commissions and over-rides you will be paid, what you need to achieve in order to promote yourself, and illustrates any other benefits which may be available throughout your Career.

Close in Booking

A date for a product presentation, which will take place within the next 6 weeks.

Collectable Products

Product ranges where items are designed to complement each other -for example a range of clothing where particular pieces work well as a 'capsule wardrobe'.

Commission

You will be paid a percentage of the sales you generate which is usually referred to as commission.

Conference

Most companies offer one or two conferences a year where they will showcase new product to be launched and offer training. Guest speakers are used for motivation and inspiration in most cases.

Consumable Products

For example: vitamins/cosmetics/candles/food.

Direct Recruit

Someone you have personally recruited.

Distributor

Name for an Independent Direct Seller. Companies used different words to describe their direct sellers including those of Retailer, Dealer, Trader and Consultant.

Downline

Team members who, according to the Career Plan, are one or more levels down from you – they may have been recruited either by you (direct recruit) or by one of your team members (indirect recruit).

Direct Selling Association (D.S.A)

A professional body which strives to raise the profile of the Industry, and to protect interests of DSA members and consumers.

Host

Person who invites others to attend a product presentation - usually in their own home.

Host Coaching

The process of coaching the person who is hosting a product presentation to ensure the success of the event.

Host Reward System

The way that (in most cases) companies reward and thank hosts for inviting guests along to a product presentation.

Incentives

Rewards offered to encourage activities in order to reach desired performance goals. Incentives are often in the form of cash bonus's/products/overseas trips etc.

Incremental Sales

These are over and above expected or required Sales. For example you may be required to sell £100 of product per week to achieve the earnings you want – if you sell £120 the £20 would be incremental.

Indirect recruits

People you have not personally recruited but have been recruited by one of your down-line.

Interview

Also referred to as a coffee meeting. This is when you meet up with someone to explain how your business works, so that they can make an informed decision as to whether to join the business.

Leads

Individuals who may have an interest in either products, or the business opportunity.

Leg

Once a team member starts to build a team of their own this is referred to as a 'leg' or a 'generation'.

Level

Your personally recruited team are your 1st level. When members start to recruit their own team, this second team become your 2nd level. When 2nd level team members recruit people, they become your 3rd level. NB. Check this out with your chosen company as it may vary!

Long-dated Booking

A Product Presentation scheduled for 6 months (or more) ahead.

Mass Market

Products sold inexpensively that appeal to the 'mass market' for example Avon Cosmetics, Kleeneze.

MLM

Multi-level Marketing is a structure by which the company rewards their team leaders for sales of others no matter how many levels down from them in the plan, whereas Network Marketing usually has a limit so may reward for perhaps just four or five levels down.

Monthly Planner

A simple calendar style form to enable monthly activities to be viewed at a glance – essentially used to plan the upcoming month's activities.

Multi-Channel

Product marketed via more than one channel. An example of which is Ann Summers who sell via Retail Outlets, Party plan and the Internet.

Non-Consumable Products

Items such as: clothing, kitchenware, household appliances, jewellery.

Overrides

Sometimes called team commissions this is a percentage of sales made by your team, in return for recruiting, training and supporting them.

Party Plan Business

Where sales are generated through parties (product presentations) made to a group of people who have been invited along by the Host.

Personal or Direct Recruits

People you have personally recruited.

Prospect

Someone who has expressed an interest in finding out about the business opportunity.

Recruiting

An activity whereby a Social/Direct seller meets with or talks to a person who subsequently joins the business – sometimes called sponsoring.

Referrals

Names of people who may be interested in product or the business opportunity, gained from customers, adverts or through general conversation with others.

Social/Direct Seller

An independent, self-employed person, who is part of the distribution system of a Social/Direct selling company. Social/Direct sellers are authorised to place sales orders from customers direct to the company. Orders are gained within a 'Social Selling Environment' such as a product presentation or social media.

Sponsor/Recruiter

This is the person who introduced you to the company.

Sponsor/Recruit

When someone new joins the business they can be referred to as a Recruit or a Sponsor.

Roll Up

This occurs when a person leaves the business - any people that they have recruited 'Roll-Up' to the person who recruited the person that has left.

Single Channel

Product marketed through one channel. For example solely through the Direct Sales channel.

Starter Kit

Usually this contains paperwork such as order forms, catalogues and general product literature in addition to a small amount of product to be used for demonstration purposes. May be referred to as a Distributor Kit.

Team Leader

Independent Direct Sellers who support a team of people, usually recruited by them. Sometimes referred to as a Manager or Director.

Team Meetings

These are for self-employed Social/Direct sellers to meet up with their peers. Usually led by the most senior and experienced seller in a team, Team Meetings are vehicles for recognition and Training.

Trunk Show

Another way of describing a product presentation whereby a Social/Direct seller takes a sample of their product range along to a host and their guests, in order to take orders and promote the business opportunity.

Up-line

The person directly above you in the hierarchy of the Career Plan. This could be the person who recruited you, or if they have left, it could be the person who was above them, as you would usually 'roll up' to that person, should your recruiter leave.

About Leigh Walton

Leigh Walton is an accomplished Direct Sales professional, having worked in the industry for over twenty five years. She started out as a self-employed 'Avon Lady' after chatting to an Area Manager who had 'cold called' at her home. Leigh attributes her first 'lesson in Social and Direct Sales' to this ad-hoc meeting as she soon came to understand that by listening to what Leigh was saying, asking open-ended questions, and then answering Leigh's needs, this Area Manager turned a 'No, I'm not interested in Avon', to a, 'Yes, I'll give it a go'!

A couple of years on, Leigh was employed as an Area Manager by Avon Cosmetics; firstly appointed to cover part of inner-city Birmingham and then the upmarket town of Solihull - 'chalk and cheese' areas, as Leigh describes them. The difference in attitude to 'Avon' in these areas tested Leigh's 'out of the box' thinking and strengthened her creativity. She is pro-active to the hilt and has also developed the ability to react positively to any given situation. After promotion to a training and development role with Avon, her career really took off.

She was soon employed by Virgin (Vie) Cosmetics for the start-up of Richard Branson's foray into 'Party Plan' and also worked with the superb book publisher, 'Dorling Kindersley', where her direct approach was welcomed by the independent sales-force. Over the next few years Leigh was approached, and subsequently recruited, by several companies including The Pampered Chef (UK) where she was promoted to National Sales Manager.

During 2012, Leigh started to make plans to fulfil her ambition of studying for an English degree, whilst also working as a self-employed Business Coach and Trainer. In April 2013 Leigh left The Pampered Chef to travel around Europe with her husband and two terriers. During this time she has also written three books and is currently studying for an Honours Degree in English Language and Literature with the Open University.

Even whilst travelling she is alert to what is happening generally 'in Sales' and whilst working her way down Croatia, upon seeing many people stood on the side of roads with large signs stating 'Apartmento', wanted to contact the agent letting her house to say, 'Have you thought of....'.

Leigh's motto of 'Life is not a Dress Rehearsal' is what drives her! In addition, a phrase learned many years ago, 'Anywhere, Anytime, Always, Ask', is one she believes all Social/Direct Sellers need to keep in adopt. Whether in a coffee shop, a queue in a shop, chatting to someone on the train, if you remember the '4 A's' you will be giving yourself the best opportunity to become a success in Social/Direct Sales.

What Are You Waiting For ?

If you have enjoyed this book why not let others know?

Please go to Amazon and leave a review!

Other Books by Leigh Walton

Social/Direct Selling - Yes You Can (Book Two)

Travels with Martha (2015)

More Travels with Martha (2015)

Katie's Diary (2015)

Letters to Sofia (2015)

The Balloon Flight & Other Short Stories (2015)

Connect with Leigh Walton

Twitter

> **http://twitter.com/@leighw10**

Facebook

> **https://www.facebook.com/pages/Leigh -Walton-Author-Writer/747679335282745**

Web Site Coming soon!

> **www.leighwalton.com**

Printed in Great Britain
by Amazon